INTRODUCING DINOSAURS

TYRANNOSAURUS REX

BY SUSAN H. GRAY · ILLUSTRATED BY ROBERT SQUIER

The Child's World®

Published in the United States of America by The Child's World®
1980 Lookout Drive • Mankato, MN 56003-1705
800-599-READ • www.childsworld.com

ACKNOWLEDGMENTS
The Child's World®: Mary Berendes, Publishing Director
The Design Lab: Kathleen Petelinsek, Art Direction and Design;
Victoria Stanley and Anna Petelinsek, Page Production
Editorial Directions: E. Russell Primm, Editor; Lucia Raatma, Copy Editor;
Dina Rubin, Proofreader; Tim Griffin, Indexer

PHOTO CREDITS
©Dmitryp/Dreamstime.com: cover, 2–3; ©American Museum of Natural
History Library (#19508): 4; ©Phil Degginger/Carnegie Museum/Alamy:
7; ©Gary Retherford/Photo Researchers, Inc.: 8 (left); ©dk/Alamy: 8–9;
©Natural Visions/Alamy: 11; ©Richard T. Nowitz/Corbis: 16–17; ©Reuters
NewMedia, Inc./Corbis: 18–19; ©AFP/Corbis: 19 (bottom)

LIBRARY OF CONGRESS CATALOGING-IN-PUBLICATION DATA
Gray, Susan Heinrichs.
 Tyrannosaurus rex / by Susan H. Gray; illustrated by Robert Squier.
     p. cm.—(Introducing dinosaurs)
 Includes bibliographical references and index.
 ISBN 978-1-60253-244-1 (lib. bound: alk. paper)
 I. Squier, Robert, ill. II. Title. III. Series.
 QE862.S3G6958 2009
 567.912'9—dc22   2009001624

TABLE OF CONTENTS

WHAT WAS TYRANNOSAURUS REX?

Tyrannosaurus rex (tih-ran-uh-SAWR-uss REHX) was a dinosaur that lived millions of years ago. Its name means "**tyrant** lizard king." Most people call it *T. rex* for short.

Barnum Brown (right) discovered the first T. Rex bones in 1902. People were surprised at how big they were.

WHAT DID *T. REX* LOOK LIKE?

T. rex was one of the biggest **carnivores** ever. It was as tall as a two-story building. It weighed as much as four cars. Its head was the size of a refrigerator.

Because T. rex *was so large, few other dinosaurs would have been a threat to it.*

T. rex had tiny arms. Each hand had two fingers. The dinosaur's legs had big, strong muscles. Its tail was thick and very heavy.

The bones of a T. rex *foot (above) would make a person's foot seem tiny.* T. rex *needed a strong body to hold up such a heavy head (right).*

9

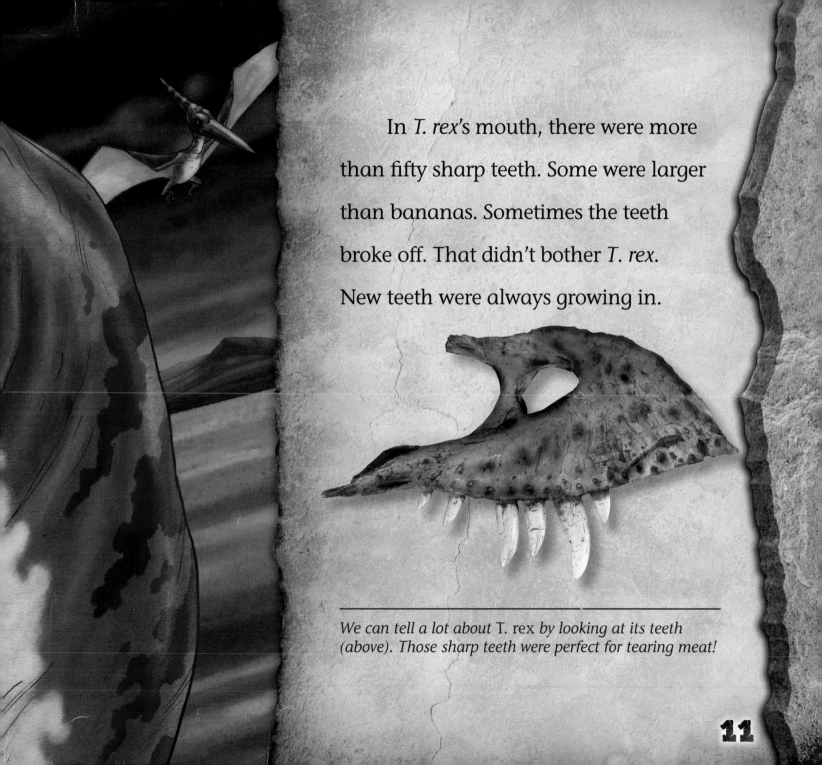

In *T. rex*'s mouth, there were more than fifty sharp teeth. Some were larger than bananas. Sometimes the teeth broke off. That didn't bother *T. rex*. New teeth were always growing in.

We can tell a lot about T. rex by looking at its teeth (above). Those sharp teeth were perfect for tearing meat!

WAS *T. REX* A HUNTER?

No one knows how *T. rex* got its food. Maybe it was a **predator**. It might have hunted and killed other dinosaurs. Or maybe *T. rex* was a **scavenger**. Perhaps it ate animals that were already dead. Either way, *T. rex* needed lots of food. It ate tons of meat every year!

Due to its huge size, T. rex *needed to eat a lot of meat. Imagine how much food a* T. rex *needed to eat in one day!*

WHAT DID *T. REX* DO ALL DAY?

T. rex spent its days looking for food and water. It also rested and took naps.

T. rex traveled by walking and running. It probably did not run very fast. If it tripped and fell, it was in big trouble. Its little arms would be crushed. Its enormous head would crash into the ground.

T. rex *had to be careful when it was looking for food. Sneaking up on its next meal was probably easier than chasing after it.*

HOW DO WE KNOW ABOUT T. REX?

Scientists have found many *T. rex* **fossils**. The fossils are often buried in the ground. Scientists carefully dig them up. As new fossils are discovered, scientists are able to learn new information about *T. rex*.

Scientists look for T. rex *fossils all around the world. Here you can see a group working along the Red Deer River in Alberta, Canada.*

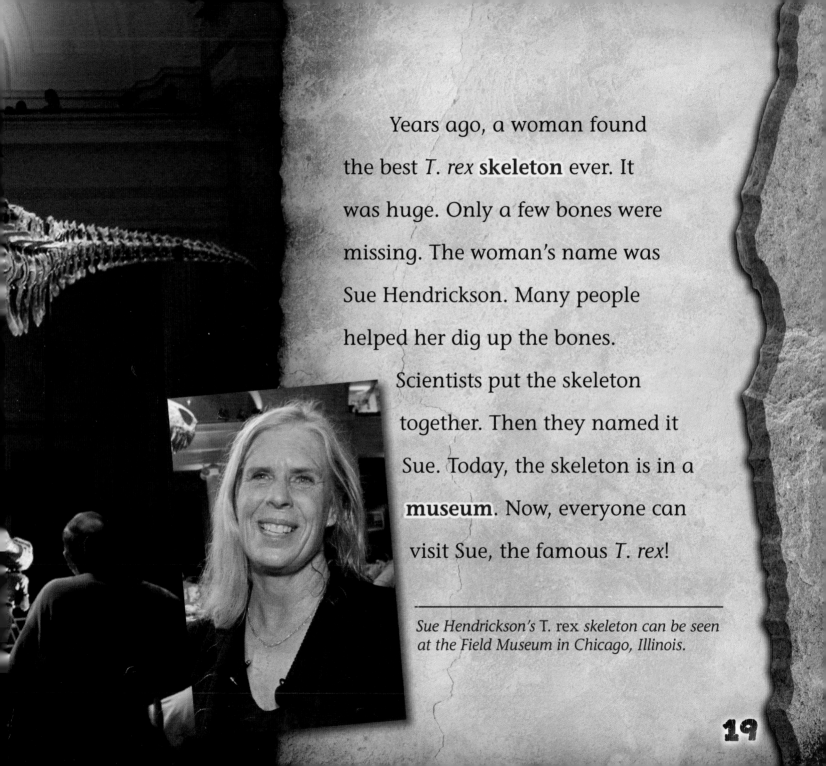

Years ago, a woman found the best *T. rex* **skeleton** ever. It was huge. Only a few bones were missing. The woman's name was Sue Hendrickson. Many people helped her dig up the bones.

Scientists put the skeleton together. Then they named it Sue. Today, the skeleton is in a **museum**. Now, everyone can visit Sue, the famous *T. rex*!

Sue Hendrickson's T. rex *skeleton can be seen at the Field Museum in Chicago, Illinois.*

19

WHERE HAVE T. REX BONES BEEN FOUND?

Saskatchewan, Canada

Montana

South Dakota

NORTH AMERICA

Atlantic Ocean

Pacific Ocean

EUROPE

ASIA

AFRICA

SOUTH AMERICA

Indian Ocean

AUSTRALIA

Map Key

Where *T. rex* bones have been found

Southern Ocean

WHO FINDS THE BONES?

Fossil hunters find dinosaur bones. Some fossil hunters are scientists. Others are people who hunt fossils for fun. They go to areas where dinosaurs once lived. They find bones in rocky places, in mountainsides, and in deserts.

When fossil hunters discover dinosaur bones, they get busy. They use picks to chip rocks away from the fossils. They use small brushes to sweep off any dirt. They take pictures of the fossils. They also write notes about where the fossils were found. They want to remember everything!

Fossil hunters use many tools to dig up fossils. It is very important to use the right tools so the fossils do not get damaged.

GLOSSARY

carnivores (*KAR-nuh-vorz*) Carnivores are animals that eat the meat of other animals.

fossils (*FOSS-ullz*) Fossils are preserved parts of plants and animals that died long ago.

museum (*myoo-ZEE-um*) A museum is a building filled with interesting things for people to see.

predator (*PRED-ah-tur*) A predator is an animal that hunts and eats other animals.

scavenger (*SKAV-un-jur*) A scavenger eats animals that have already died.

scientists (*SY-un-tists*) Scientists are people who study how things work through observations and experiments.

skeleton (*SKEL-uh-tun*) The skeleton is the set of bones in a person or animal's body.

Tyrannosaurus rex (*tih-ran-uh-SAWR-uss REHX*) *Tyrannosaurus rex* was a big dinosaur that lived millions of years ago.

tyrant (*TYE-runt*) A tyrant is a very cruel ruler.

BOOKS

Bentley, Dawn. *Snack Time, Tyrannosaurus Rex!*
Norwalk, CT: Little Soundprints, 2004.

Landau, Elaine. *Tyrannosaurus Rex.*
New York: Scholastic, 2007.

My Terrific Dinosaur Book.
New York: DK Publishing, 2008.

Parker, Steve. *Dinosaurus: The Complete Guide
to Dinosaurs.* New York: Firefly Books, 2003.

WEB SITES

Visit our Web site for lots of links about *Tyrannosaurus rex*:

CHILDSWORLD.COM/LINKS

*Note to Parents, Teachers, and Librarians: We routinely verify our Web links to make
sure they are safe, active sites—so encourage your readers to check them out!*

INDEX

ABOUT THE AUTHOR

Susan Gray has written more than ninety books for children. She especially likes to write about animals. Susan lives in Cabot, Arkansas, with her husband, Michael, and many pets.

ABOUT THE ILLUSTRATOR

Robert Squier has been drawing dinosaurs ever since he could hold a crayon. Today, instead of using crayons, he uses pencils, paint, and the computer. Robert lives in New Hampshire with his wife, Jessica, and a house full of dinosaur toys. *Stegosaurus* is his favorite dinosaur.